GLACIERS

Nature's Icy Caps

David L. Harrison

Illustrated by
Cheryl Nathan

Boyds Mills Press

The author wishes to thank Erwin J. Mantei, Ph.D., Professor of Geology, Southwest Missouri State University, for his review of the text and illustrations.

Text copyright © 2005 by David L. Harrison
Illustrations copyright © 2005 by Cheryl Nathan
All rights reserved

Published by Boyds Mills Press, Inc.
A Highlights Company
815 Church Street
Honesdale, Pennsylvania 18431
Printed in China

CIP data is available

First edition, 2006
The text is set in 14-point Optima.
The illustrations are done digitally.

Visit our Web site at www.boydsmillspress.com

10 9 8 7 6 5 4 3 2 1

For Robin, whose smile would melt any glacier
—D. L. H.

For my good friend, Deborah Davey
—C. N.

In 1912 no ship was mightier
than the *Titanic*.
But its first voyage ended in disaster.
Titanic struck an iceberg and sank.
The giant ship was no match
for a giant chunk of ice from a glacier.

Most icebergs in the North Atlantic
split off from glaciers in Greenland.
It was one of these glaciers
that sank the *Titanic*.
Snow in Greenland gets so deep
that snow below is pressed into ice.
The ice grows thicker and heavier
until its great weight
makes it inch downhill.
When ice starts to move,
it becomes a glacier.

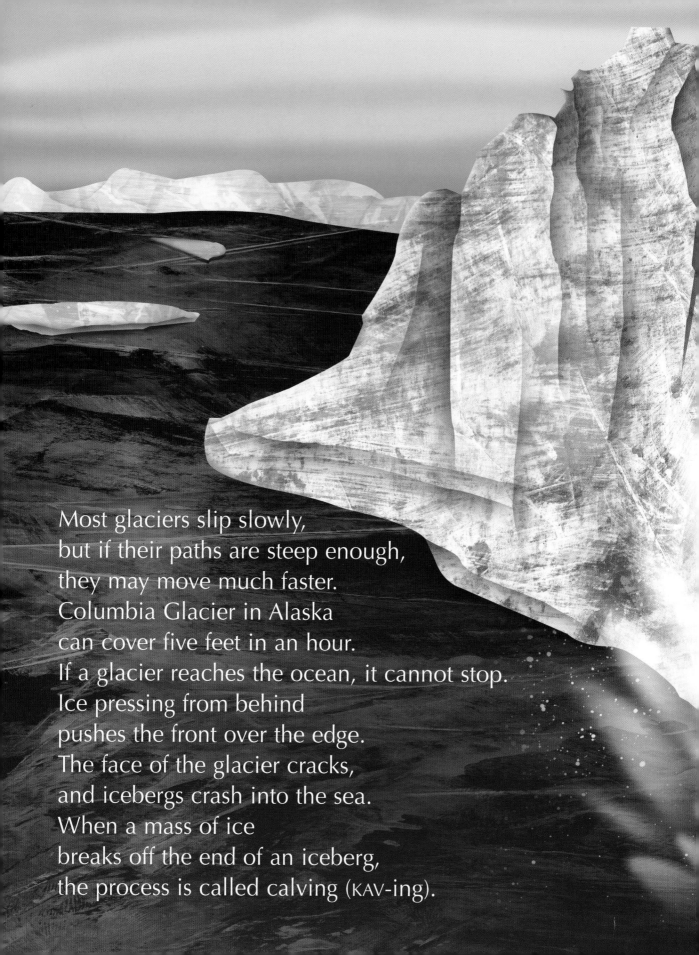

Most glaciers slip slowly,
but if their paths are steep enough,
they may move much faster.
Columbia Glacier in Alaska
can cover five feet in an hour.
If a glacier reaches the ocean, it cannot stop.
Ice pressing from behind
pushes the front over the edge.
The face of the glacier cracks,
and icebergs crash into the sea.
When a mass of ice
breaks off the end of an iceberg,
the process is called calving (KAV-ing).

A glacier may take
thousands of years
from the time it forms
until it reaches the sea.
Iceberg ice may be older
than pyramids in Egypt.
Most of that ancient ice
melts in two or three years.
By then some icebergs
drift for thousands of miles.

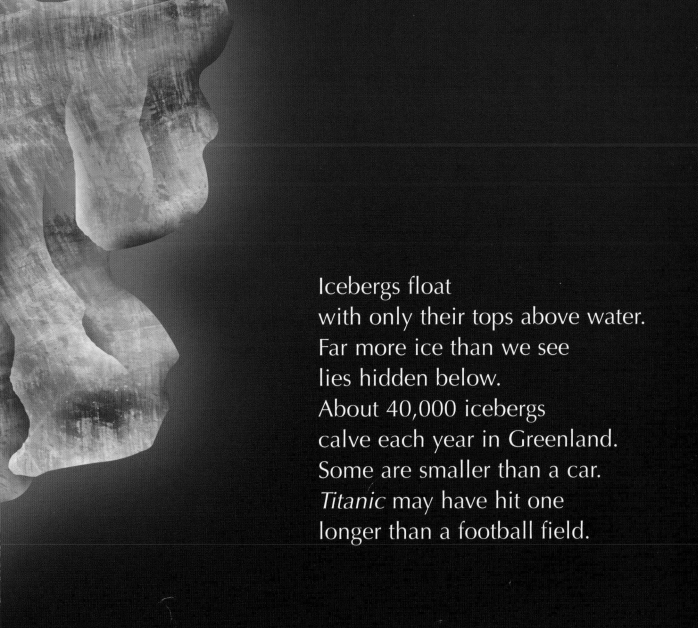

Icebergs float
with only their tops above water.
Far more ice than we see
lies hidden below.
About 40,000 icebergs
calve each year in Greenland.
Some are smaller than a car.
Titanic may have hit one
longer than a football field.

The largest glacier is found
on the coldest place on Earth.
Lambert Glacier in Antarctica
is five times bigger than Nebraska.
Most of Antarctica lies buried
under ice more than one mile thick.
There is so much ice,
it grows for miles beyond the coast.
The biggest icebergs
calve from those huge shelves.

Alaska may have 100,000 glaciers.
But not all glaciers make icebergs.
Many hang high
in mountains and valleys
and never reach the sea.
Near the equator in Africa,
mountain peaks hold glaciers
while lions roam the hot plains below.

A glacier thousands of feet thick
weighs millions of tons.
Its mighty force
gouges valleys deeper and wider.
It flattens forests
and grinds boulders into powder.
As the glacier creaks along,
it polishes stone
and leaves deep grooves
like marks of monster claws.

A glacier grows as long as it gets
more snow than it loses.
When the air turns warm,
the glacier starts to shrink.
Water frozen for thousands of years
melts into icy rivers
and roars down valley walls.
Earth and boulders freed at last
dam up pools to form lakes.
Muddy dirt and rock powder
stain the water many colors.

Earth goes through cycles
of warming up and cooling off again.
The cycles last about 100,000 years.
A cool time is called an Ice Age.
During the last Ice Age,
much of North America
and parts of Europe and Asia
lay under thick sheets of ice.

When ice captures
so much water
from rain and snow,
ocean levels drop.
Land may appear
where water used to be.
During the last Ice Age,
Asia became connected to Alaska.
Animals and people
could walk to North America.
We call the land they
crossed Beringia.

As time passed, Earth warmed up
and the Ice Age ended.
By 10,000 years ago,
the great sheets of ice
were shrinking and melting away.
Water from glaciers ran into oceans
and made them rise.
Once again the ocean covered Beringia.
We call that part of the sea
the Bering Straight.

At the end of an Ice Age,
melting glaciers also flood the land.
It takes a long time
for so much water to disappear.
Low places may fill up as lakes
like the Great Lakes
in North America.
Frozen ground thaws again.
Plants begin to grow.
Animals return.

Today Earth is warming.
Many glaciers are melting.
But thousands of years from now,
Earth will again turn cool enough
for monster glaciers to form.
Sheets of ice miles thick
will cover parts of the planet
and ocean levels will drop.
But that Ice Age will also end
like all the ones before it.
The more we learn,
the more we understand
that nothing on Earth
stays the same forever.

AUTHOR'S NOTE

Each book in the Earthworks series introduces a complex subject about Earth at an introductory level. In seven hundred words, I attempt to provide a clear text with basic information to whet the appetites of young readers. Other titles suggested by librarians are listed to encourage the pursuit of additional information.

Glaciers and ice fields more than one mile thick wield incredible weight and power. Earth's crust bears scars, cuts, and deepened valleys gouged by glaciers sliding and grinding down mountains toward lower places. The weight is enough to depress Earth's surface. So much water stored as ice causes ocean levels to drop. Climates change. Plants and animals perish or take refuge (for thousands of years) in safe havens high above the frozen fields. At the end of an Ice Age, water floods the land. Oceans rise and spill over the coasts until the crust regains its shape and drains off the sea. Climates adjust. Living things reestablish their habitats and migrate toward new sources of food.

The vast ice fields of Greenland and Antarctica were there long before the last Ice Age, but as big as they are they can only hint at the scope of the ice that crept down North America 20,000 years ago all the way to Missouri. The great glaciers of the last Ice Age are nearly gone. Scientists generally agree that the Ice Age ended 10,000 years ago, but glacial melting began thousands of years earlier and continued into modern times. What remains of those icy giants are scattered, ghostly reminders of the past.

Here's something even more astonishing. In spite of global warming and short-term temperature fluctuations, Earth is already headed into the next Ice Age! Someday new ice sheets will march southward and cover much of the land that we call the United States. But don't stock up on gloves yet. The coming Ice Age is thousand of years away.

— **David L. Harrison**

FURTHER READING

Nadeau, Isaac. *Water in Glaciers.* New York, N.Y.: PowerKids Press, 2003.
Tangborn, Wendell V. *Glaciers.* New York, N.Y.: Harper and Row, 1988.
Walker, Sally M. *Glaciers: Ice on the Move.* Minneapolis, Minn.:
    Carolrhoda Books, Inc., 1990.